We Asked For Nothing

The Remarkable Journey of Cabeza de Vaca

FOR JOSH

Editor: Elizabeth Mann
Design: Lesley Ehlers Design

Library of Congress Cataloging-in Publication Data

Waldman, Stuart, 1941–
    We asked for nothing : the remarkable journey of Cabeza de Vaca/ by Stuart Waldman;
illustrated by Tom McNeely.
    p. cm.–(A great explorers book)
    Summary: An Account of the travels of the Spanish explorer Cabeza de Vaca through Texas
and Mexico from 1528 through 1536, looking particularly at his relations with the native
people with whom he shared his journeys.
    Includes bibliographical references and index.
    ISBN 1-931414-07-6
    1. Núñez Cabeza de Vaca, Alvar, 16th cent.—Juvenile literature. 2. America—Discovery
and exploration—Spanish—Juvenile literature. 3. America–Description and travel—Juvenile
literature. 4. Indians, Treatment of—History—16th century—Juvenile literature. 5. Indians
of North America—History—16th century—Juvenile literature. 6.
Explorers—America—Biography—Juvenile literature. 7.
Explorers—Spain—biography—Juvenile literature. [Cabeza de Vaca, Alvar Núñez, 16th
cent. 2. Explorers. 3. America—Discovery and exploration—Spanish. 4.
 Indians—Treatment. 5. Indians of North America—History—16th century.] I.
McNeely,
 Tom, ill II. Title. III. Series.

E125.N9W35 2003
970.01'6'092--dc21

                                                                          2003046472

Printed in China

We Asked For Nothing

The Remarkable Journey of Cabeza de Vaca

By Stuart Waldman

Illustrated by Tom McNeely

MIKAYA PRESS

NEW YORK

"We asked for nothing but gave away
all that we were given, while the others
seemed to have no other aim but to
steal what they could and never
gave anything to anybody."

From *La Relación*,
by Alvar Núñez Cabeza de Vaca

Red River

Brazos River

Colorado River

San Antonio River

Río Grande

Texas

Apalachee

ATLANTIC OCEAN

Culiacán

Sierra Madre

Matagorda
Bay

Malhado
(Galveston Island)

FLORIDA

Padre Island

Tampa Bay

PACIFIC OCEAN

NEW SPAIN
(Mexico)

GULF OF MEXICO

Mexico City

CUBA

HISPANIOLA

THE JOURNEY OF
CABEZA DE VACA
1528-1536

Keep the other side
of this page open.
You can read about
Cabeza de Vaca's travels
and follow them on the
map at the same time.

In 1492 a native chief on the Caribbean island of Hispaniola gave Christopher Columbus a belt with a golden buckle. It was one of several signs of the precious metal that Columbus saw during his voyage. The following year he returned to the New World with seventeen ships and twelve hundred men. Some came to establish colonies. Some came to bring the word of God to the people Columbus called "Indians." Most came for the gold. Over the next thirty years, hundreds of Spanish ships sailed west filled with young men seeking their fortunes. They were called conquistadors—conquerors.

Conquer they did. The Indians that resisted were slaughtered. Those that didn't resist were enslaved. They worked the fields and searched for gold under the most brutal conditions. Hundreds of thousands perished.

Most conquistadors viewed Indians as little more than animals and were unconcerned with their suffering. Others were troubled. The pope had ordered Christianity spread to native people. If they were beasts, how could they also be Christians?

Spanish priests who had been to the New World witnessed Indian suffering firsthand. A few began speaking out and their words reached the king. Laws were enacted to protect Indians, but most conquistadors, living thousands of miles from Spanish justice, ignored them. From time to time, the king would appoint officers in the New World to report on the conquistadors' treatment of the native people. One of these men was Alvar Núñez Cabeza de Vaca.

"Are they not men?... Are you not obliged to love them as yourselves? By what authority have you waged a detestable war against these people?"

—

FATHER ANTONIO
DE MONTESINOS,
PREACHING
TO A CONGREGATION
OF CONQUISTADORS.
HISPANIOLA, 1511

In 1527 King Charles V made Cabeza de Vaca second in command of an expedition to the New World led by Pánfilo de Narváez. The king ordered Cabeza de Vaca to report on "how the natives are treated."

Cabeza de Vaca knew nothing of natives. He was a soldier, descended from generations of soldiers. He had been fighting in European wars since he was a young man and was now in his mid-thirties. The Narváez expedition was his chance to become rich. If an Indian stood between him and gold, there was every reason to believe that Cabeza de Vaca would behave like any other conquistador.

In April of 1528, Narváez's four ships dropped anchor in what is now Tampa Bay, Florida. In a nearby Indian village, the Spaniards came upon small pieces of gold. They demanded to know where they could find more. Communicating through sign language, the Indians told them that the gold came from a village called Apalachee. They said it overflowed with treasure, but it was inland and very far to the north of Tampa Bay.

This presented a problem for Narváez. The Spaniards would have to march a long way to Apalachee, and once there they might have to fight hostile Indians. If they ran out of food and water, they would be too far from their ships to resupply.

Narváez decided that while he led his soldiers north by land, his ships would sail north. His soldiers would then have only a short march from Apalachee to their ships.

Narváez threatened and abused Indians to get information from them. Cabeza de Vaca never raised an objection.

The three hundred heavily armored men slogged for months through Florida's steamy, mosquito-infested swamps searching for Apalachee. When they finally found it, there was no gold. Either the Indians at Tampa Bay had been mistaken or they had lied so the menacing strangers would go as far away as possible.

Meanwhile, many of the Spaniards had become ill from the heat and tropical diseases. The maize (Indian corn) they'd stolen from villages along the way was nearly gone, and Indian warriors continually ambushed them from the safety of the forest. More than fifty Spaniards died.

They hurried to the coast only to find that their ships weren't there. Their captains had found no harbor on the north coast and had been forced to turn back. Narváez and his ragged army were trapped between Indian arrows on one side and the Gulf of Mexico on the other.

Their only hope was to build boats and sail out of trouble. They melted the iron from their stirrups, spurs, and crossbows and used it to make primitive saws, axes, and nails. They cut down palm trees for wood. They ate their horses and braided their manes and tails into ropes and rigging. They wove their shirts together to make sails. In this manner, five small, bargelike boats were constructed, and nearly fifty men were jammed into each one.

They sailed west toward New Spain, which is now called Mexico. It had been conquered by Hernán Cortés in 1519 and there were Spanish settlements throughout the country. Narváez's charts had indicated that New Spain was only forty-five miles away, and he was confident they'd be there in a few days. What he didn't know was that his primitive charts were terribly wrong. New Spain was actually over nine hundred miles away!

During the following months, the boats drifted apart on the vast Gulf of Mexico. On November 6, 1528, Cabeza de Vaca's boat was alone, off the coast of what is now Texas. The men had been without drinking water for days, and their food supply was down to a handful of raw maize for each man.

As the boat edged closer to land, a large wave tossed it into the air. It hit the water with a jolt, shot forward, and skidded to a stop. The exhausted men climbed out and crawled through the mud onto a beach. They found pools of rainwater and gulped it down greedily from cupped hands. They gathered driftwood and cooked the last of the maize. They huddled around the meager fire.

"We had been suffering from hunger for so many days and had been pounded so much by the sea that the following day many men began to faint....All the men in my boat had passed out, one on top of the other, and fewer than five were still upright."

FROM *LA RELACIÓN*, BY ALVAR NÚÑEZ CABEZA DE VACA

Cabeza de Vaca ordered Lope de Oviedo, the strongest of his men, to climb a tree. From the top he shouted to his commander that they were on an island. He saw paths but no people. A short while later a hundred Indians walked silently out of the woods. They were naked and each of them carried a bow and arrows.

Cabeza de Vaca cautiously approached the Indians and presented them with shiny beads and little tin bells. The Spaniards had brought the trinkets to trade for gold, but now they were trading for something far more precious—their lives.

The Indians seemed pleased. Each one solemnly handed Cabeza de Vaca an arrow in return. He believed, or at least hoped, that it was a sign of friendship.

The next morning the Indians, members of the Karankawa tribe, returned with food and water. In the afternoon Indian women and children, adorned with their new beads and bells, came to gawk at the pale-skinned creatures who covered their faces with hair and hid their bodies beneath strange coverings. Every day the Karankawa returned with more food and water.

"A hundred Indian archers appeared and our fright was such that whether tall or little, it made them appear like giants to us....We could not even think of defending ourselves, since there were scarcely six men who could stand on their feet."

FROM *LA RELACIÓN*, BY ALVAR NÚÑEZ CABEZA DE VACA

When they had stored enough supplies, Cabeza de Vaca gave the order to resume sailing to New Spain. By now the tide had pushed their boat onto the beach where it lay half buried in the sand. They spent much of the morning digging it out. It was backbreaking work and the sun was hot. Soaked with sweat, the men stripped off their clothes and threw them in the boat. With their last bit of strength, they pushed it into the water and climbed in.

They rowed furiously to get past the breaking surf and into calmer water. They had almost made it when a wave washed over them. The shock of the icy water on their naked bodies caused them to drop their oars. At that instant an even larger wave hit. Out of control, the boat flipped over like a toy and sank to the bottom of the sea. Three Spaniards drowned.

When the Karankawa returned to the beach that evening, they were shocked to see the Spaniards, as naked as they themselves were, seated next to the bodies of their drowned comrades. It was an autumn night on an open beach. The sun had set and a frigid north wind was blowing. The Spaniards shivered violently. Without clothes to cover their emaciated bodies, the Indians saw their true condition for the first time. They looked at the three corpses and at the forty-six men who were barely alive, and they began to weep. Their mournful cries echoed over the water.

"The rest of us, as naked as we had been born, had lost everything, and while it was not worth much, to us it meant a great deal....
We were in such a state that our bones could easily be counted and we looked like the very image of death."

FROM *La Relación*, by
ALVAR NÚÑEZ CABEZA DE VACA

The Karankawa lifted the Spaniards as easily as if they were sticks of driftwood and carried them inland. Fires were lit every few hundred yards along the way and the Indians stopped at each fire to warm the Spaniards. They continued from fire to fire for a mile and a half, until they reached their village.

As the Spaniards lay snugly inside a large hut, they heard the Indians singing and dancing. They couldn't sleep. It wasn't the noise of celebration that kept them awake. It was fear. Some of the men had served in New Spain and had heard stories of human sacrifices. The Spaniards believed the Indians were celebrating because they were about to sacrifice them.

The Karankawa had shown them nothing but friendship. They had fed them, wept for them, warmed them, and sheltered them, but none of that mattered. To the Spaniards, Indians were savages and not to be trusted.

The next morning the Karankawa brought more food and water. They also brought news. Another boat from the Narváez expedition had capsized further north on the island. All the men aboard had survived. Hours later Captains Andrés Dorantes and Alonso del Castillo embraced Cabeza de Vaca in a joyful reunion.

There were now eighty-nine Spaniards on the island. Their boats were at the bottom of the sea, and they had neither the tools, the materials, nor the strength to build new ones. The only way they could make it to New Spain was to walk. That would be difficult enough, but it was impossible without first crossing to the mainland. The Karankawa had canoes but they wouldn't go to the mainland until February when they harvested oysters in the many bays along the coast. In the meantime, the Spaniards were stranded.

That winter was a terrible one. Driving rain and high winds pounded the island. The storms were so violent and so unrelenting that the Indians rarely left their huts to find food. Already severely malnourished, the Spaniards began to die, one by one. By the time the storms abated, there were only fifteen left alive. They named the island "Isla de Malhado"—Misfortune Island.

Many of the Indians had also become ill that winter. They were weary of the strangers who seemed to have brought nothing but bad times with them. The Indians demanded that they do something useful and ordered them to heal the sick. The request was so outlandish that Cabeza de Vaca thought they were joking. To show how serious they were, the Karankawa stopped bringing them food.

Having no choice, the Spaniards went to the huts of the sick Indians. They recited the Lord's Prayer and made the sign of the cross. They also bent down and blew on the Indians' bodies as they'd seen Karankawa medicine men do. All the Indians they "treated" said they felt better. The bearded strangers were now seen as powerful medicine men performing a valuable service for the tribe. They were given food even if it meant some of the Karankawa had to go hungry.

By February the months of starvation had taken their toll on Cabeza de Vaca. He lay in a Karankawa hut more dead than alive. Two other Spaniards, Jerónimo de Alaniz and Lope de Oviedo, were also seriously ill. Dorantes and Castillo were certain that the three men were dying and that if the rest of them remained on Malhado they would die as well. When the Karankawa crossed to the mainland, twelve Spaniards, led by Dorantes and Castillo, went with them. They began the long walk to New Spain.

Alaniz died but Cabeza de Vaca and Oviedo both recovered. Perhaps because their comrades had deserted them or perhaps because they had become ill themselves, they had lost the respect of the Karankawa. They were no longer seen as medicine men and had to do real work if they wanted to eat. Cabeza de Vaca was assigned the job of gathering swamp potatoes, a root that grew in shallow streams among fields of razor-sharp reeds. As he reached underwater to pull out the stubborn roots, the reeds cut his naked body. It was an exhausting, unpleasant job and, although Indian women did it every day, Cabeza de Vaca considered it slave's work. He decided to leave Malhado.

He crossed to the mainland and began living with a new tribe, the Chorruco. Cabeza de Vaca knew little about the mainland Indians, so he watched and learned. He observed that trade was an important part of life on the mainland, but when the tribes were at war, which was often, all trading stopped. As an outsider, Cabeza de Vaca was not involved in tribal wars and was the one person who could move freely between all tribes at all times. This endlessly resourceful man saw his opportunity. He became an Indian trader.

THE KARANKAWA

"Of all people in the world they are the ones who love their children most and treat them best; and should the child of one of them die, the parents and kinfolk and the whole tribe weeps for him, and their lamentation lasts for a full year, day after day....they mourn all their dead, old people excepted, saying that these have had their time and are no longer of any use, but only take space and food from the children."

FROM *LA RELACIÓN*, BY ALVAR NÚÑEZ CABEZA DE VACA

He traveled hundreds of miles a year, through hot summers and harsh winters, walking from village to village barefoot and without clothes. From the coastal tribes he gathered sharply pointed snail shells that the Indians used as cutting tools. He brought these to the inland tribes and in return received items like red ochre used for face paint and flint used for arrowheads. He was welcomed in every village because he brought goods that were needed.

Despite his success, Cabeza de Vaca never stopped thinking of home. He returned to Malhado and asked Lope de Oviedo to go with him to New Spain. Oviedo might have been younger and stronger than his captain, but he was far more timid. He had remained on the island because, as difficult as life was with the Karankawa, he knew he was safe with them. Out on the trail, anything could happen.

Cabeza de Vaca would not leave a fellow Spaniard behind, nor did he want to attempt the long journey by himself. Once a year, he returned to Malhado to plead with Oviedo. He assured him that he would not be harmed by the Indians. All the tribes—the Chorruco, the Deaguane, the Mendica, the Queuene, the Acubado, the Quitole, the Maliacone, the Camole—knew and respected Cabeza de Vaca. He had mastered six Indian languages, knew their customs, and had learned where their trails led. He even promised to carry Oviedo across the rivers along the way since the younger man couldn't swim.

THE MAINLAND TRIBES

"There are those who quarrel and have disputes among themselves, they strike and beat each other to the point of exhaustion and then draw apart....No matter how angry they are they do not resort to bows and arrows in these fights. And after they have pummeled each other and had out their dispute, they take their houses and their wives and go live in the plains away from the others until their anger has cooled. And when they have overcome their animosity and are no longer angry, they return to their village and from then on are friends as though nothing had happened between them."

FROM *LA RELACIÓN*, BY
ALVAR NÚÑEZ CABEZA DE VACA

In 1533, Cabeza de Vaca's persistance was finally rewarded. More than five years after Lope de Oviedo climbed the tree in Malhado, he crossed to the mainland. The two men followed the trail west until they reached a large body of water known today as Matagorda Bay. They were now at the end of the territory in which Cabeza de Vaca had traded. Beyond this point, he knew little of the land or the people.

They met a band of Queuene who warned them that if they continued along the trail, they would come upon the Maraeme and Ygauce, two extremely dangerous tribes. They were sure to attack the Spaniards, and if they didn't kill them, they would enslave them. In fact the Queuene had recently met three Spaniards who were being held as slaves by the Maraeme and Yguace. They were Captains Andrés Dorantes and Alfonso del Castillo and Estebanico, a North African slave who had served on the Narváez expedition. The three men were the only survivors from the twelve who had left Malhado for New Spain.

Lope de Oviedo's worst fears about mainland tribes were confirmed. He turned around and headed back to Malhado. Cabeza de Vaca didn't hesitate. Alone and unarmed he strode into a Maraeme village.

He was captured and enslaved. He had expected this. Once in the village, he planned to meet with the other Spaniards and organize an escape. It turned out to be far more difficult than he'd imagined. The four men were held in two separate villages and were rarely together long enough to speak with each other, much less stage an escape.

Time passed. If Cabeza de Vaca's life in America had been hard, now it became unendurable. It wasn't only the beatings and death threats. The Maraeme and Yguace lived under conditions that were as brutal as they were. Cabeza de Vaca had become accustomed to hunger, but nothing like what he found among these Indians. The Maraeme and Yguace often went three or four days without eating, and then they would eat anything to survive: spiders, ant eggs, worms, dirt, wood, even animal dung.

It was only in the summer, when the prickly pear cactus was in bloom, that these wretched people were assured of food. The cactus grew in abundance in the arid southwest and to the Indians, its small, bumpy, purplish fruit was a gift from the gods. The prickly pear harvest was a time of great celebration. The Maraeme and Yguace danced day and night while gorging themselves on the precious fruit.

A year and a half after Cabeza de Vaca walked into slavery, the Maraeme and Yguace came together for a prickly pear harvest. Cabeza de Vaca knew that this might be his only chance. He met with Castillo, Dorantes, and Estebanico and on September 14, 1534, while the Indians were celebrating, the four men slipped out of their huts and ran to freedom.

They fled west, moving quickly for fear that the Maraeme and Yguace would follow them. Toward evening they saw smoke from a village. After all they had been through, they were understandably cautious. They had no idea what tribe lived in the village, whether they would be welcomed or enslaved, but they had been walking all day under a blistering sun. They moved toward the smoke.

THE MARAEME AND YGUACE

"All the Indians in the land are their enemies with whom they are always at war; and if by any chance their enemies should marry their daughters, their enemies would increase so much they would conquer and take them as slaves. Hence they prefer to kill their daughters rather than see them give birth to children who would become their enemies.…When they want to get married, they buy their wives from their enemies."

FROM *LA RELACIÓN*, BY ALVAR NÚÑEZ CABEZA DE VACA

The village was home to the Avavare, who gave the Spaniards a welcome beyond their wildest dreams—and for the most unlikely of reasons. Somehow the story of the bearded strangers who had cured the Karankawa more than six years before had found its way to the Avavare. When they saw the Spaniards, they were certain that healers had walked into their village.

The Spaniards were given food and water and huts to rest in. Then the Avavare didn't let them rest. That night Indians lined up outside Castillo's hut complaining of headaches. He made the sign of the cross and blessed them. The Indians said their heads felt better. The next day the Avavare celebrated the coming of the new medicine men. The Spaniards were served a feast of prickly pear and, most wonderful of all, venison.

Word spread to nearby tribes. Cutalchiche, Maliacone, Coayo, Susola, and Atayo all came to see the Spaniards. The Indians would arrive complaining of illness and depart proclaiming that they were cured. Soon the Spaniards were taking care of more than headaches. One night they made the sign of the cross over five Avavare who had been crippled by illness. The next morning all five awoke and walked.

"We never treated anyone who did not say he was cured. They were so confident that our cures would heal them that they believed none of them would die as long as we were there."

From *La Relación*, by Alvar Núñez Cabeza de Vaca

The crippled Avavare walk.
How was this possible?
Different people would have
different explanations.
The Indians believed that the
Spaniards were shamans—
people who traveled to the
spirit world and returned with
magical powers.

Cabeza de Vaca believed
that God healed the Indians
so that they would help the
Spaniards survive.

Moderns doctors know that
patients who believe strongly in
their treatment can have the
symptoms of their illness
disappear—at least temporarly.
At present there is no scientific
explanation for this.

A legend was born that winter. The Indians began calling the four men the Children of the Sun because they believed that they had come from the heavens.

The Spaniards continued their journey, and the legend went with them. In villages all along the trail, Indians lined up to be blessed and healed. Some left their homes to follow the Children of the Sun. In one large village they were greeted by hundreds Indians rattling stone-filled gourds and beating their hands rythmically against their thighs. After being blessed every single person left their village and joined the growing procession.

They crossed the Rio Grande and then turned west to avoid the tribes living along the coast who the Spaniards had heard were violent. They then moved north skirting the highest peaks of the Sierra Madre mountain range. The trail meandered through the high plains, a heavily populated area. Every day more Indians streamed from their villages to join the healers. Soon nearly four thousand people were following the Children of the Sun!

It was an extraordinary sight. Old men and women, young warriors, little children, mothers carrying newborn babies—the line stretched for miles along the winding trail. The four Spaniards looked little different than the people they led. They were naked except for the ragged deer skins around their waists. Their backs and chests were pockmarked with sores from wind-driven sand. Their feet were crisscrossed with scars from walking barefoot through cactus fields.

THE INDIANS OF NEW SPAIN

"They have no pots, so to cook they fill half a large gourd with water. They put many stones into a fire and when the stones are burning hot they grab them with wooden tongs and throw them into the water in the gourd, until they make it boil with the heat from the stones. When they see that the water is boiling they throw into it whatever they want to cook."

FROM *LA RELACIÓN*, BY
ALVAR NÚÑEZ CABEZA DE VACA

Hunters went into the hills and returned in the evening laden with deer and birds. Thousands of Indians sat down on the open plains and waited as the day's kill was placed before the Children of the Sun. The Indians had been walking on the trail all day, but until the food was blessed, not one person would touch it.

All four men were constantly healing, but the busiest was the leader, Cabeza de Vaca. Always a religious man, his beliefs had deepened during his years in the New World. For Cabeza de Vaca, the healing of the Indians was proof that God had blessed the Spaniards. He was certain that, with God's help, he could heal any Indian who came to him.

Once he even performed surgery on a man who had an arrowhead wedged near his heart from an old wound. Using a deer bone knife, he cut through the skin and carefully pulled the arrowhead out. He stanched the bleeding with deer hide and stitched the wound closed. The Indians had never seen anything like it. Cabeza de Vaca gave them the arrowhead and it was passed from tribe to tribe like a holy relic, more evidence of the power of the Children of the Sun.

"We all became healers because so many people insisted, but I was the boldest and most daring in undertaking any cure....For myself I can say that I always had hope in God's mercy and knew that He would bring me out of captivity, and I always said this to my companions."

FROM *LA RELACIÓN*, BY ALVAR NÚÑEZ CABEZA DE VACA

The procession approached the last mountains of the Sierra Madre. The Indians began drifting back to their villages, wary of hostile tribes that might be on the other side of the mountains and hoping to make it home before winter. The Spaniards continued west, climbing rocky trails in their bare feet. There were few villages at this altitude, and they often went hungry.

When they finally crossed the mountains, the trail turned south just before it reached the Pacific Ocean. This was the land of the Pima and Opata tribes, and, compared to where the Spaniards had been, it was a land of plenty. Here the Indians grew their own food and filled storehouses with maize, flour, squash and beans. Here they harvested fish from the Pacific Ocean, hunted the abundant deer that grazed in lush meadows, and lived in sturdy, permanent homes made of sun-baked mud.

Yet even the Pima and Opata, living thousands of miles from the Avavare, had heard of the Children of the Sun. They lined up to be blessed in every village, but the Spaniards would not remain in one place for long. They were deep into New Spain, and they knew there had to be Spanish settlements nearby. They moved south, always looking for a sign of their countrymen.

One day, in a small Indian village, they saw a buckle from a Spanish sword belt. Trying to appear calm, they asked where it had come from. The Indians described men who had beards like the Children of the Sun, but who had come on horses and carried swords and lances.

THE PIMA AND OPATA

"We saw women more modestly arrayed than in any other part of the Indies that we had seen. They wear cotton skirts that reach as far as the knee and over them deerskin tunics, with strips that hang to the ground.... they wear shoes."

FROM *LA RELACIÓN*, BY ALVAR NÚÑEZ CABEZA DE VACA

They praised God and raced down the coast where they found far more disturbing signs of Spaniards. Villages were deserted. Homes were burned to the ground. Fields of maize were choked with weeds. A few Indians wandered around in a daze, so hungry they ate the bark off trees. They told Cabeza de Vaca of men who came on horseback, setting fire to their homes, abducting men, women, and children. Entire villages had fled to the safety of the mountains in fear of these men.

Cabeza de Vaca took Estabanico and eleven Indians with him. Following the hoofprints of the soldiers' horses, they walked day and night through rugged terrain until they came upon four mounted men in full armor. Heavy swords hung from their waists, and in their right hands they held long, pointed lances. They stared at Cabeza de Vaca for a long time, speechless at the sight of the gaunt, nearly naked man, accompanied by a black man and leading a group of savages. It must have been even more confusing when Cabeza de Vaca spoke. In perfect Spanish, and with the authority of a king's officer, he asked to be taken to their captain.

"We traveled far and found the entire country empty because the people who lived there were fleeing to the mountains, not daring to work the fields or plant crops. It was very pitiful for us to see such a fertile and beautiful land filled with water and rivers, with abandoned burned villages, and to see the people who were weakened and sick, all had to flee and hide."

FROM *LA RELACIÓN*, BY ALVAR NÚÑEZ CABEZA DE VACA

A week later the Children of the Sun, along with hundreds of Indians, stood before Captain Diego de Alcaraz. Cabeza de Vaca had persuaded the Indians to leave their hiding places and face the man who had destroyed their world. He had asked them to bring maize and blankets, which he then gave to Alcaraz and his soldiers. If he expected the captain to be grateful for the Indians' generosity, he was mistaken. Alcaraz demanded that the Indians be handed over to him to be sold as slaves.

King Charles V had once commanded Cabeza de Vaca to safeguard the liberties of people like these. The words had meant little to him then, but everything had changed. He had lived with Indians for eight years. He had learned their languages and their customs. He had worked with them, suffered with them, depended on them, and survived because of them. Through it all, he had come to see native people in a far different way than when he had begun his journey. Like all people, some were good, some were evil, some were cruel, some were kind, but there was one thing of which Cabeza de Vaca was now certain: Indians were human beings, children of God, and not animals to be bought and sold.

Cabeza de Vaca and Alcaraz began shouting at each other. Alcaraz then spoke directly to the Indians. He told them that the men they had followed were not gods. They were Spaniards, like him, only they were cowardly and unlucky and had been wandering around lost for a long time. Diego de Alcaraz was lord of this land and the Indians must go with him.

The Indians conferred and then told Alcaraz that he was a liar. The Children of the Sun could not be Spaniards, because they weren't thieves and murderers.

Alcaraz became enraged. Why he didn't kill them all will never be known. Perhaps he thought the story would get out and he would be hanged for the murder of Spanish officers. Or perhaps he was stunned by the fact that, in the company of Cabeza de Vaca, the Indians were unafraid of him.

The meeting broke up. The Indians retreated to the safety of the mountains. The Children of the Sun walked ninety miles until they reached a Spanish settlement, San Miguel de Culiacán. There they met with the mayor, Melchior Díaz, who repeatedly wept and gave thanks to God as he listened to Cabeza de Vaca's story of hardship and survival. When he heard of the confrontation with Alcaraz, he became upset.

Melchior Díaz had recently arrived in New Spain and was a loyal officer of the king. He knew that enslaving peaceful Indians and destroying their villages went against the king's laws, but Díaz also knew he couldn't simply arrest Alcaraz. The captain had a powerful friend, the governor of the province, Nuño de Guzmán. He was a vicious conquistador who hated Indians and encouraged Alcaraz's raids. Mayor Díaz had to find a way to stop Alcaraz without angering the governor.

THE INDIANS' RESPONSE TO ALCARAZ

"We {the Children of the Sun] healed the sick and they {Spanish soldiers] killed the healthy. We went naked and shoeless and they wore clothes and went on horseback and with lances. We asked for nothing, but gave away all that we were given, while the others seemed to have no other aim but to steal what they could and never gave anything to anybody."

From *La Relación*, by Alvar Núñez Cabeza de Vaca

He came up with a plan that was both simple and bloodless. He would convert the Indians to Christianity. The pope had forbidden the enslaving of Christian Indians. Díaz hoped that Alcaraz would not defy his church as well as his king.

A week later, Cabeza de Vaca and Díaz met with three chiefs who had come down from the mountains at his request. Cabeza de Vaca asked them to whom they prayed when they wanted water for their fields. A man in heaven called Aguar, they replied. Cabeza de Vaca said the Christians called Aguar God and told the Indians they must do the same. Melchior Díaz then gave the Indians a choice: if they became Christians, all Spaniards would regard them as brothers and they could return to their land. If not, they would be carried off into a life of slavery. The Indians said they "would be good Christians and serve God."

When Alcaraz's soldiers entered Indian villages, they were welcomed with crosses. They saw churches being built and children being baptized. Alcaraz ordered his men to leave the Christian villages in peace.

The Indians' safety assured, Cabeza de Vaca was ready to go home. The Children of the Sun left Culiacán for New Spain's capital, Mexico City. They were given clothes, but they were so accustomed to going naked that it would be weeks before they put them on their bodies. They spent their nights in Spanish homes, but they were so unused to beds that they slept on the floor. When they arrived in Mexico City, they were welcomed as heroes by Hernán Cortés himself.

Not wanting to cross the ocean during the winter months, Cabeza de Vaca did not leave New Spain until April. Finally in August 1537, ten years and two month after the Narváez expedition left for the New World, Cabeza de Vaca arrived home.

The country he returned to was much like the country he had left. Francisco Pizarro had conquered Peru in 1532 and sent the gold of the Incas back to Spain. New expeditions were organized, headed by men dreaming of being the next Pizarro.

In his own way, Cabeza de Vaca shared these dreams. Like most Spaniards, he never questioned Spain's right to the Indians' land or their gold. He also believed that Christians had a duty to convert native people. Even conversion under threat of slavery, as Melchior Díaz had done, was justified because the Indians' souls would be saved.

Where Cabeza de Vaca differed from the conquistadors was in his attitude toward native people. He believed that if Indians were approached with gentleness and understanding, they would embrace Christianity and turn into loyal subjects of the king. He saw himself as a new kind of conquistador, one who would conquer without killing, who would colonize without enslaving.

This kind of thinking appealed to King Charles, who was genuinely pained by the injustices of his conquistadors. In 1540 the king appointed Cabeza de Vaca governor of the Rio de la Plata (River of Silver), an enormous territory encompassing what is now southern Peru, Argentina, Uraguay, and Paraguay. The Spanish believed there were great riches in Rio de la Plata, but, because of continuous fighting between conquistadors and South American tribes, exploration had been limited. Cabeza de Vaca's task was to win over the Indians and put a stop to the fighting.

He failed in every way. He removed some enslaved Indians from the worst masters, but he was not able to end slavery entirely. Even if he had, he would have not won the support of all the Indians. There were South American tribes who wanted nothing to do with Spain or

"One can clearly recognize that all these people, in order to become attracted to becoming Christians and subjects of your Imperial Majesty, needed to be treated very well; this is the sure way to accomplish this; indeed, there is no other way."

FROM *LA RELACIÓN*, BY
ALVAR NÚÑEZ CABEZA DE VACA

Christianity. To them Cabeza de Vaca was simply another Spaniard at the head of an army, taking over their land.

For their part, the conquistadors of Rio de la Plata despised Cabeza de Vaca for what they saw as his softness toward Indians. They revolted in 1544 and Cabeza de Vaca was sent back to Spain in chains. He was charged with a variety of offenses including robbery and corruption. The charges were never proven, but the conquistadors had powerful friends in the Spanish court. The king, perhaps disappointed in Cabeza de Vaca for his failures in South America, did not defend him. He was eventually set free, but spent the rest of his life trying to clear his name. Cabeza de Vaca died sometime after 1556. The former hero had become so unimportant that the year and place of his death went unrecorded.

He was not forgotten in the New World. In 1582 an expedition led by Antonio de Espejo arrived at an Indian village near the Rio Grande. Upon seeing the Spaniards, the Indians asked to have the sign of the cross made over their women and children. Espejo was puzzled. He was in unexplored territory, far from any Spanish settlement, among people who had never seen a European, much less heard of Christianity. Espejo asked the Indians where they had learned of the cross. This is what they told him, nearly fifty years after the journey of the Children of the Sun:

"Three Christians and a black man passed that way.... Through them God showed many miracles, and they healed, only by the touching of their hands, many sick persons and became very famous in all the country."

EPILOGUE

Upon returning to Spain in 1537, Cabeza de Vaca wrote a book about his eight years in the New World. Few read La Relación (The Account) during his lifetime, but more than 450 years later, this little hundred-page book has come to be considered one of the more important works from the Age of Exploration.

La Relación is many things. It is an adventure story, a tale of hardships and dangers, hair-raising escapes, and ultimate survival. It is also a story of discovery. Cabeza de Vaca was the first European to set foot in Texas and the Children of the Sun's twenty-five-hundred-mile walk covered areas that weren't on the maps of his time. Cabeza de Vaca's descriptions of this unknown landscape helped in the planning of future expeditions, while the length of his journey proved that America was indeed a vast continent.

In the end Cabeza de Vaca's greatest discovery was not a land, but a people. If he knew nothing of Indians when he left for the New World, he returned an expert. Entire chapters of La Relación *are devoted to rich and detailed descriptions of the daily life of the native people of the southwest: their customs, rituals, celebrations, what they ate, where they lived, how they hunted, traveled, married, raised children, fought, and died.*

Most of the tribes with whom Cabeza de Vaca came in contact have long since disappeared. Although Spanish attitudes slowly changed and laws protecting natives became better enforced, it was too late. Diseases such as smallpox, which had been unknown in America, were brought to the New World by Europeans. In some areas as many as 90 percent of the Indians died from the new diseases. The tribes that survived were forced to adapt their culture to that of their conquerers.

In La Relación *we see the Indians of the southwest as they were before the arrival of Europeans, their ancient way of life as yet unchanged. Cabeza de Vaca did not save them but because of him they live for us.*

THE NARVÁEZ EXPEDITION

At the same time that the two boats landed on Malhado (thought to be today's Galveston Island), a third boat landed farther south on what is now Padre Island. The men were attacked by Indians and all forty-five Spaniards were killed.

A fourth boat was wrecked near Matagorda Bay. The crew survived and began walking along the beach. The last boat, commanded by Narváez, landed safely on the same beach and joined up with the other crew. Narváez argued with one of his officers and remained on his boat that night. A sudden storm drove it out to sea. He was not seen again.

The eighty survivors spent the following months wandering along the Texas coast. Avoiding Indians, they were unable to find food during that same harsh winter that Cabeza de Vaca endured on Malhado. By the end of March, only one man was left alive, Hernando de Esquival. He was captured by the Maraeme, enslaved, and eventually killed.

Lope de Oviedo was never seen again.

NEW SPAIN

DIEGO DE ALCARAZ returned to enslaving and slaughtering native peoples. In 1541, he was killed by warriors from the Sobapauri tribe.

GOVERNOR NUÑO DE GUZMÁN was removed from office for disobeying the king's commands, particularly in his cruelty toward Indians. He was imprisoned for two years and then sent back to Spain, where he died, in 1544, penniless and in disgrace.

MELCHIOR DÍAZ became a captain in Francisco Vásquez de Coronado's famed expedition to the American southwest. He died in 1541, accidentally speared by his own lance.

The Children of the Sun

ANDRÉS DORANTES remained in New Spain. The viceroy, New Spain's highest official, arranged a marriage for Dorantes with the wealthy widow of a conquistador. Dorantes raised four children and lived the rest of his life in comfort as the master of his wife's estates.

ALONSO DEL CASTILLO also married a rich widow. He served in important government positions: judge, the royal inspector of Guatemala, and, for a brief time, governor of Mexico City.

ESTABANICO'S fate was the most interesting and the saddest. He had come to the New World as Andrés Dorantes's personal slave. Throughout the journey of the Children of the Sun, Estabanico had served as an advance scout and was often the first to go into villages to make contact with new tribes. Despite the services he had performed and all that he had endured, Dorantes didn't free him. In 1537, he sold Estabanico to the viceroy who had heard of his skills in communicating with Indians and wanted him to guide expeditions into Indian territories.

In 1539, Estabanico was the advance scout for an expedition to Zuni Indian territory in the far north. He approached what he had been told was one of the seven cities of Cibola. Cibola was a legend among conquistadors, said to have "streets lined with goldsmith shops, houses of many stories, and doorways studded with emeralds and turquoise!" Estabanico entered the Zuni village and was met with a shower of arrows. He died on the spot.

The village, like Apalachee twelve years before, contained no treasure.

INDEX

SOURCES

Adorno, Rolena and Pautz, Patrick Charles, *Alvar Núñez Cabeza de Vaca: His Account, His Life and the Expedition of Pánfilo de Narváez*, University of Nebraska: Lincoln, 1999.

Bandelier, Fanny (Translator), *The Journey of Alvar Núñez Cabeza de Vaca and His Companions from Florida to the Pacific, 1528-1536*, A.S. Barnes: New York, 1905.

Bishop, Morris, *The Odyssey of Cabeza de Vaca*, The Century Company: New York, 1933.

Favata, Martin A. and Fernandez, Jose B., *The Account: Alvar Núñez Cabeza de Vaca's Relación*, Arte Publico: Houston, 1993.

Hallenbeck, Cleve, *Alvar Núñez Cabeza de Vaca: The Journey and Route of the First Europeans to Cross the Continent of North America*, Kennikat: New York, 1971.

Howard, David A., *Conquistador in Chains: Cabeza de Vaca and the Indians of America*, University of Alabama: Tuscaloosa, 1997.

Morison, Samuel Eliot, *The Great Explorers: The European Discovery of America*, Oxford University Press: New York, 1978.

Thomas, Hugh, *Conquest: Montezuma, Cortes and the Fall of Old Mexico*, Simon & Schuster: New York, 1993.

Wood, Michael, *Conquistadors*, University of California: Berkeley, 2000.